THINK DEEP

BEFORE YOU THINK BIG

- **Develop innovative thinking power and gather essential knowledge through a casual reading to rule the corporate world.**
- **Lucid and simple to read and imbibe.**

FOR
SALES AND MARKETING
PROFESSIONALS AND ENTREPRENEURS

SUBRATA HALDER

BlueRose ONE.com
Stories Matter

First Published in June 2022

ISBN: 978-93-5628-143-1

BLUEROSE PUBLISHERS
www.BlueRoseONE.com
info@bluerosepublishers.com
+91 8882 898 898

Cover Design:
Geetika

Typographic Design:
Namrata Saini

Distributed by: BlueRose, Amazon, Flipkart

"It is better to light a candle than to curse the darkness."

Confucius

About The Author

I know Subrata for more than twenty years. The first thing that comes to my mind is that he is a very nice human being and has a great helping attitude and ethical values. He has a strong passion for art, writing and painting. He is professionally an engineer, but he writes, I used to read his stories in top Bengali magazines including the most prestigious The Desh magazine. He got several awards also when he was in Kolkata. I am happy that he restarted writing and surely he will contribute good articles and write ups relevant to our society, especially to the youngsters. My best wishes for his future endeavours.

Prof. (Dr) Dhrubajyoti Chattopadhyay,
Vice Chancellor, Sister Nivedita University
Ex ProVC Calcutta University

I have known Subrata for twenty years now. Always righteous, with high integrity and an absolute idealist, he was my first learning how a technical person acquires this huge customer trust and intimacy. Those days, back in Kolkata, not a single customer wasn't his best friend. He loved them crazy, and they reciprocated. His other trait that impressed me, back to that day, is his deep intellectual creative prowess. He was the first medical device professional I knew who was an acclaimed author and playwright. His creations were already greeting published in very reputed publications. Over the past two decades, I have seen Subrata morph, especially this past ten years, through which I have only seen him from a distance. I have watched him grow in his professional career and at the same time, seen with a lot of admiration, his paintings. I see this book by Subrata as another testimony of his relentless expression; this is perhaps one more effort from him to contribute and help others. I wish him well always; I wish his book good readership and I wish the readers good learning. May Subrata continue to excel in his pursuits.

Probir Das
Group Executive Officer - Terumo Corporation-Japan,

Subrata always prioritises values like honesty and ethics in a very competitive sales world but wins most of the time. His team loves him because of his sincerity and wide-ranging life sciences market knowledge including minute technical matters which automatically generates an effective motivated team and makes him an effective leader. Teachers make leaders and Subrata lives it daily like a habit. He is an extremely talented writer, but innovation lies in his deep understanding of human nature. Subrata has developed great strategic thinking in marketing and has successfully turned strategy into action & execution in a few very tough assignments. He has gained positively from his experience which has provided him with agile strategic ability.

Sunit Trivedi
Ex. Managing Director, Beckman Coulter & Ex. Director, Becton Dickenson

Subrata is simple. He will never cheat you. His personality is silk smooth. He is a writer, painter, and cook. He has a unique quality of teaching other as well as sharing good things with others be it painting, writing or critical management/ marketing and life lessons. Most importantly expressing critical matters in simple forms, at times a storytelling manner is his speciality. I'm sure, Subrata's book on Marketing would be simple, clear and thought-provoking. I'd be eager to read the book to celebrate our 20 year long-distance friendship.

Professor Abhijit Chakrabarti

Senior Scientist, Saha Institute of Nuclear Physics.

Subrata, always addressed by friends as 'Dada' stands out from the crowd sustaining a routine life of job & home. An epitome of creativity in professional & personal life, being truthful and with fearless conduct. His expression of creativity in the form of writings & paintings captures realities of life & nature. Subrata's such qualities substantially contemplate his professional aura.

Dr Arvinder Singh

Country Manager, India, Human Diagnostics GmbH

To my love…CHOKO….

the youngest member of our family

Contents

PREFACE

Think big is the most used phrase in the last few decades with the boom of entrepreneurship. There are dozens of books on this subject. Think big remains on the tip of the tongue of the leaders, entrepreneurs, and motivational trainers.

Think big is good but equally bad if not supported by thinking deep. This is the reason why most of the big ideas either fail or struggle for a long time. There may be many examples of the success of big thinking but those are supported by a great amount of deep thinking which usually comes through experience, panoramic knowledge, and the power of analysis. Only subject knowledge does not help. The most important is business knowledge when it is a business-related project. This is the reason the majority of start-ups fail though backed by highly educated technology people. Because marketing and selling in business are most important which often get neglected. I tried to capture several aspects of sales and marketing looking from a different angle. Also, some lifestyle elements are important for every individual to be successful in their professional assignment, which is captured in a few articles. Because of the versatile subject matters, the reading will not be monotonous but enjoyable.

As mentioned, thinking deep requires panoramic knowledge but more importantly, the habit of thinking deep needs to be cultivated. Innovative thinking and thinking differently are important for deep thinking which is again a most spoken phrase but seldom practised.

This is not a book which is an accumulation of marketing theories. Such information can be available plenty in book form and on websites. Here I tried to cover many aspects in my own writing style, mostly storytelling mood, which are important to be successful in sales & marketing job. As well as to provoke deep thinking which is important not only for the professions but to lead a nice personal and family life.

I have tried to write in lucid language so that it is not only easy to understand but easy to imbibe. If we read something to learn, it is less effective compared to if we read for the joy of reading.

All articles in this book are completely my own thoughts that come from three decades of experience and good power of observation. However, as this is my first book, you may find some mistakes and pardon me for that as I am also learning book publishing by this way. I wish day by day I shall move toward perfection.

I believe all of you will enjoy reading this book and appreciate it. Also, it will be a great help for me if you write a short review (comment or suggestion) on Amazon/ Flipkart or on the sites from where you bought this book. Thanks for your support.

LET US PLAY SALES...

Newcomers in the sales profession go through professional training and often fail to embrace the heavy jargons surfeit to them like leads, qualify, funnel, cold calls, capability building, development plan, skill, strategy, tactics, game plan, slowdown, success, teamwork, growth, FoS, KPI, IIG et cetera. An easy way to understand this is to relate it with some passion and build passion in a new dimension.

One can relate it with many of his/her passions. I could see a unique resemblance between two of my fascinations which may be true for many others. One, as an avid lover and division player of football and the other, on compulsion, is sales, where I parked my career. I feel the fusion of thought may be interesting for budding sales representatives. Easy to understand and to store in the pleasure centre of grey matter. Let me explain on a lighter note.

Territory:

We can play football only within a certain demarcated area. The same is true for sales, we need to play in a certain demographic area. Keep the ball in your territory. Dribbling out of the territory can result in an offensive throwback against your interest. True when we are selling.

Competitions:

The rule of the game is to have a compulsory opponent. Selling too goes with this, that is called a competitor. The most difficult hurdle before success, but one has no other choice in most of the situations. All strategies revolve around beating them. Important to respect their ability and never to underestimate them. As well as they are not enemies. All are following their objectives, that is all. Today's competitor can be tomorrow's friend. The world (read market) is too small to make an enemy.

Goal:

In football, three bars of the goalpost are visible. Same way the goal of the organisation and the goal of the individuals should be clear and visible. All strategies and hard work are to penetrate through the defence and cross the target goal line. A goal may not be always an order but smaller steps to accomplish the final objective that is the order or maximise win.

Skills:

The best team and best players do not guarantee success. The best product or best prices are not the best criteria but the best sales skills are. Developing Individual competency plays a crucial role for the team. Today's excellent knowledge and skill can be not sufficient for tomorrow so continuous learning and improvement is important. Or there can be a paradigm shift of the technology and/or market which demands completely different knowledge and skill to be successful.

Success:

Success is not how good one played but how many goals a team scored. Similarly, in sales, success has primarily numbered a team or individual achievement. However, in football, if the opponent scores more; then even after scoring several goals one team has to accept defeat. Is not this the same in sales? If the number is not adequate or below the market growth of that geography, does it not win or deserve appreciation? If competitors grow faster, then is it a notable success? So, success is relative and not an absolute quantity. Achieving a rightly set objective is a success. Here the rightly also can be dynamic with time. So, the mid-term objective setting is very common.

Rules:

The most painful moment for the supporter or players is when a team scores a goal and within a moment gets rejected because of off-side rules or foul play. It is equally important in sales. Know the rules before you slide your team jersey. Rules are usually not negotiable. More importantly, the rule of the land, rule of the institutes, demographic area, related to products etc need to be known as they may vary. Following the rules not only mitigate risk but bring peace of mind (for self and an organisation). Ironically the majority of sales and marketing people I have observed are not aware of the rules which is dangerous for the organisation. You may find some of the tender rules in my article in this book 'selling high value…'. However, that is just a small piece of a large pie. Need own study the way we study technologies and other subjects.

Preparation:

Preparation should start with the analysis of the situation and defining the strategy accordingly. The intention is to cross the opponent players. This is not possible using the same skills. It may fail as the opponent is also preparing to defeat your best skills. In sales, it is important to practice & use different skills & styles. The need is to improvise new styles beyond the competitor's imagination.

Fair play:

Mother of all rules. Be careful about Red-Cards. Any deleterious act not only damages an individual's reputation but puts the team in trouble for the game and next. Also, it is especially important in business. The slightest greed or unfair aggression can jeopardise the entire organisation's reputation and plan. Players are to kick and dribble the ball and not to kick the opponent or dribble with ethics.

Groundwork:

It is important to have clarity on the strength, weaknesses, and strategies of the opponent team. Environment and field conditions also matter. Positioning of defence and offence critically depends on it. Without background information, the so-called best strategy can revile the worst one. No difference in sales. Market intelligence is a continuous process and needs to be as accurate as possible.

Strategy & Tactic:

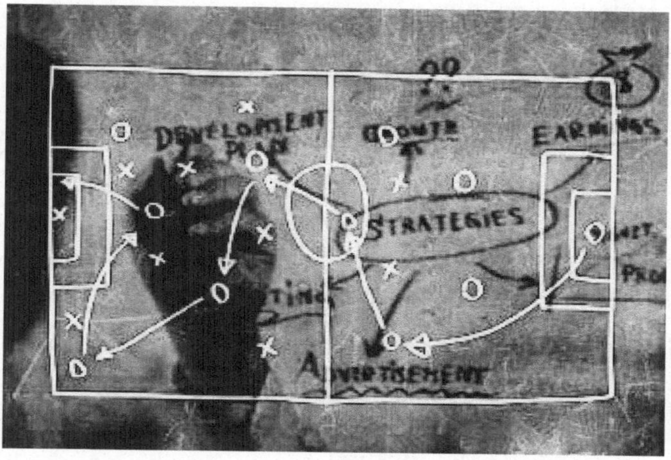

Football is a ninety-minute game for spectators. But it is months and years of practice for players to create an appropriate strategy and to design the best tactic to plan the win.

Sales closing can be a matter of one meeting. But planning starts much earlier with proper strategy & tactics. Here in addition to it market development, creating needs are also included.

Clarity on Ws (who, when, why, what, where) helps to define the best strategy and a clear vision of H (how) helps to make the best tactic. The best tactic can make a stronger opponent weaker. One can blow up an opponent by efficient use and tactical positioning of the powers in the game as well as in sales.

Challenge the limit:

I can't do it. They are stronger. They get better facilities and are more equipped. They are the market leaders. Are these not common concerns? Cameroon repeatedly proved these as excuses and could beat the world's so-called best teams for years having no facilities but challenging their own limits. At times it is very important to find one reason which can help to win than hundreds of reasons not to.

Teamwork:

Most spoken phase in football & in sales. Easy to say, but difficult to achieve in reality. Not really difficult if leaders are aware of the common challenges behind achieving teamwork and how to mitigate those challenges. Every individual works to see his/her work get appreciation. A leader needs to ensure this. It is clearly visible in football. The goal is the goal but the goal-getter is not the one who always gets the best appreciation. Lionel Messi, Cristiano Ronaldo, Zinedine Zidane, Platini or Baichung Bhutia are usually not the highest scorers always but are famous for their passes where the striker had nothing to do other than to doze the ball in the net.

In sales also the team has to be designed in such a way that the sales team or any individual only should not be always in the limelight, but all contributors get the appropriate appreciation and personal benefits. Without good teamwork, a team can do some miracles sometimes but can't reach their desired goal and sustain.

Team building:

Coach and managers never play infield but they are the most important persons behind the win.

Scolary, Parreira, Zagallo never played top-class football but were among the best coaches in history. It is said that a coach is as good as his team. But the coach is the person who actually creates the team. There are numerous examples of the highest budgeted teams, full of talented players miserably failing for the want of a proper guardian who can extract the best performance from an individual as well as form strong bonding between players. Leaders play this most vital role in sales to get the best performance out of every individual with full clarity & flexibility.

Positioning of players:

Position your players first. Decide how to design an attack. By wings or middle? Who will lead the attack? This not only depends on your available strength but the strength and weakness of the opponent.

Who will lead the game; marketing, sales or service team is equally important. Every game is unique and the last strategy/win may not work well in the next game/project.

Control the game:

Keep the ball in your control. There are situations where opponents deploy all players to defence. It is difficult to crack their rock solid wall. The team often uses a tactic of slowdown and plays within a team in their own half. Not to lose control of the ball. With this tactic, the opponent gets frustrated or complacent and starts diluting their defence. Once the team sees the hole in the wall of the opponent, they speed up and destroy the defence with a blitzkrieg. The slowdown is not really slow but a strategy to get results fast.

Apparently looks like a slowdown can't be an option in sales with MQY targets. Not the revenue slowdown but the withdrawing force from dry areas, strategic focus on potential areas with limited resources is an option. It can be true for some products from the extensive range at times. Also, it can be against competitor's unsustainable offers & price throws. Small sacrifice for grabbing bigger opportunities. Sometimes to avoid orders which can bleed the organisation. Useful to buy time. The slowdown can be a good option against hard negotiation too.

Swerve shot:

The goalkeeper is complacent because the ball is going far away from the posts. Suddenly, to everyone's surprise, the ball starts bending toward the posts leaving no time for others to prevent the loss. Making opponents complacent is a unique strategy when one is confident in his skills. But do not underestimate the wind direction (shift of customer's perception) and field condition.

Opportunistic:

Everyone knows that Paolo Rossi was not a very skilful player. But he is among only a few in history who won all three top awards in football. He scored three goals in the quarter-final, two goals in the semi-final and one goal in the final in the 1982 World cup for Italy which itself is a all times record. These six goals helped the team to win the World cup in 1982 beating more competent opponents. He won the Golden Boot as top scorer, Golden Ball as the best player of the tournament and Best European Footballer of the year, all in the same year. His best quality was to remain near the goal box and not miss the slightest opportunities. No one knew him before 1982 world cup tournament. God helps brave and probably opportunistic people too with some wise & strong desire. It works.

Being close to customers always and keeping an eye on opportunities can help one beat a so-called bigger player in sales. Also one should not to underestimate any of the team members. Good leaders understand that "not so skilful players" like Rossi etc have other qualities which can be more deadly against competitors.

Beat all concepts:

One can if he/she is extraordinary. The almost mythical Diego Maradona is regarded as the God of football by many like me. He singlehandedly pulled a humdrum team to win the World cup in 1986 against highly rated competitors like Germany and Brazil defeating them all by his extraordinary performance. In sales, it is called relation. Nothing works better than relation. Relation helps to win in spite of not the best product or lowest price. However, like Maradona, it requires decades of hard work, fair deal to elevate self as 'Resourceful Expert' to 'Loyal Champion' and ultimately a 'Trustful Advisor'. No shortcut is possible in this process but is possible only through ethical deeds spread over years.

Play till the last whistle:

Many teams had to accept defeat when they were very close to win and showed a sluggish attitude at the last moment. The last-minute goal is a common phenomenon in football. Can you connect with your bad or good experience in sales? Never give up or be complacent. Sale is not complete till shipment (invoiced). anything can happen in spite of the order being ensured or even in hand in this fiercely competitive environment. It can be vice versa as you can convert a loss to a win. Do not shift your focus and follow every movement of the ball in sales too.

Celebrate:

Celebrate the win with all. A team should have a nice jamboree after the big one. People who are not in the field could have played a big role in the win. Give credit to all. But this is not end. This is the start of the next. Get ready, be steady again and go.

Next event:

You can't climb the ladder of success with your hands in your pockets - Arnold Schwarzenegger

You won. You elevated yourself one step. Stretch your hands. Prepare yourself for the next one. Must be a tougher one and this is the beauty of the sports. Again you need to Win. The show must go on.....

Sales is not only product knowledge and/or market knowledge. Need to think deep and act deeper to win, especially when a salesman handles high ticket items or big orders.

SELLING HIGH-VALUE PRODUCTS

Distinctive in India and the Subcontinent

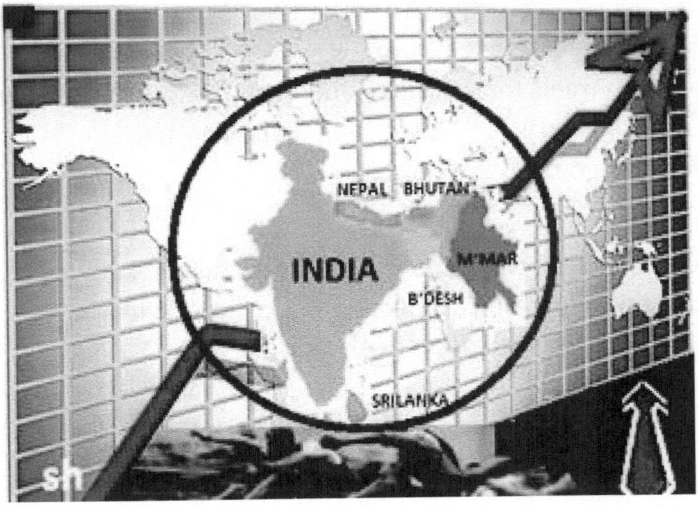

Selling is an art. Selling requires skills. But most importantly selling requires knowledge. It is not only about product knowledge but also the process knowledge. Knowledge about the mentality and attitude of customers, rules, regulations and legal terms. These are unique in every demographic region and ever-changing. So, I know, is not all but continuous learning is important.

So, here I am describing what is unique or distinctive in India in the buying & selling process which are a must-know for any person or organisation doing business in India. However, the discussion is mostly based on my long experience of selling and marketing scientific products in India but a few fundamentals can be the same for other product and customer segments.

Selling in India and the subcontinent is unique in nature unlike many other parts of the world. In retrospect, some self-experience and a myriad observation is the base of the article. Analysis of opportunities and tips to overcome practical challenges as below can be beneficial for the people actively engaged in selling.

For better understanding, I would like to divide the discussion into two parts. One is selling in Government organizations and the other is the Private sector. Selling to private organisations is relatively straight forward however selling in a government organisation is required to satisfy a lot of rules and regulations and some of those are a century old.

Here government purchase of scientific products is mostly purchased by the institutes (research and health care) funded by CSIR, DBT, DST, ICMR, ICAR, DAE and MoH and procurement is directly by Institutes or through RITES, HLL & State Health Organisations etc.

Mostly high-value government purchases are tender based unlike in western countries. In western countries, users are allowed to buy what he/she wants in a very trustworthy environment, mostly. But in India & subcontinent 'purchaser' decide. Purchaser comprises of the user, procurement department and in some cases external agencies. Also, it goes through a rigid tender process. Mostly the user has the liberty of choosing the right product limited to defining the specification. But the liberty is curbed heavily for high ticket items as the user needs to ensure several companies (minimal three) can bid and a minimum of two bids are technically qualified for price comparison. It is difficult for high-tech items to find a common ground where several companies can quote as only a few companies worldwide manufacture such items. So, the user has the risk of diluting specification too much and therefore ends up getting a poor system that does not serve the purpose. If the user wants a very specific product to satisfy the application's needs, then the user has to go through a time-consuming process of re-tendering the same for three times. Alternatively, he/she has to go for a proprietary product but it is difficult to find true proprietary features in most of the situations. Also, this carries the risk of challenging the specification by other parties jeopardising the entire process. One wrong understanding about proprietary specification/ feature is, that it should not be a technical feature only but should substantially satisfy the unique application which can't be possible to perform without this feature.

So, considering these factors what should be the practical approach for the sales team to escalate the rate of healthy wins?

1. **Building relations** – the most important part for the win is building fair and trustful relations by building the confidence at all levels of the purchaser that the company is not a selling organization but a trustful partner for long-term cooperation and benefits. Needless to mention that it is not easy to build trustful relations as it needs the highest level of inherent (not imposed by training etc by the company) honesty and a pro-customer approach at all times. I feel honesty comes from family and a company can teach do's and don'ts only. Neither relationship can be built overnight nor can a good reputation of decades be spoiled by unfair players.

It is important to keep in mind that a once satisfied customer is not guaranteed to remain satisfied or loyal forever in the present dynamic world. Therefore, it is necessary to devise formal and informal feedback mechanisms to assess customer sentiments and to take corrective action accordingly.

2. **Setting expectation and specification** – Though the ultimate goal is setting the right specification, the approach

should be through exploring benefits. We need to know the goal of user before setting a sales goal. We need to understand the field of work, present and future application, and desire and then to match the benefits out of the features of the product vs the needs (strong & desire) of the user. Selling specifications/ features is a weak approach that can be beaten by others. However, selling benefits helps customers stick to their decision. Also, the major advantage is that the customers feels confident and can comfortably justify their fair decision to the purchase committee and others. One needs to keep in mind, what can be the USPs and strategies of all other competitors. This requires in-depth knowledge of their own product as well as all competitors' products. However, remember not to be too aggressive.

The setting specification is not limited to hardware only. It applies to reagents, consumables, chemicals etc too and sensitivity, hardware match, longevity, clone, etc help to set lock-in specifications.

Here is a catch. I have seen that many of the sales team members are not aware of all the unique features of their own products. I believe all companies have their own system to train the team. However, for high-tech products, the core competence of the sales guy (front-line sales representative and first-line manager) is very important. Otherwise, no effort can deliver the desired result. So, it starts right from appointing the right guy. The right guy does not mean the disqualification of a particular guy, the person can be excellent in another field. Right guy means how he/she is fit for a particular assignment. This is a commonly ignored area that jeopardizes the sale.

The best strategy to sell the benefits is proper teamwork. Not only can it cover up the shortfall of one individual but also is unavoidable in any condition. One needs to take direct help of the product, application and at times of the service support members. This not only helps to set the right specification, which is the ultimate goal of a salesman but also boosts the goodwill of the organization.

3. **Dealing with dignity** – There are no shortcuts and no alternative to dealing with dignity. The caustic fact is to acknowledge that the environment in this subcontinent is not fair as it should be. One can blame as many people as he/she wants but I believe the sellers should demonstrate integrity. Many may find this comment surprising as sellers feel comfortable to think that they are the victim of the situation but this is untrue.

I want to assert from experience that in this small world one can successfully sustain for decades by building a solid reputation achieved through a strict ethical approach. It also helps to get panoramic support and great peace of mind in work besides respect. This is the ultimate mantra to win, grow and sustain.

4. **Bid preparation** – it is not uncommon that after doing great work for years a silly mistake in bid preparation can throw all good work to junk. The key is to avoid overconfidence, to do things systematically and to have multiple people check and recheck the artefacts.

There are several common things in each tender case. One is the submission of statutory documents of the organization such as registration, ST clearance, licenses, Installation list, user's satisfaction certificate etc. One needs to always keep the latest one handy and not to start collection against tender as one may not have enough time once the tender is published. Also s/he sometimes needs to depend on other department colleagues who may take their own sweet time.

The other vital point is cross-reference. Especially when several technical data sheets are enclosed, the cross-reference of each point should be mentioned and highlighted clearly. In the comparative sheet, sellers should mention the document type, page and line against each specification. Never anticipate simple things are known to all so not to mention. Because it is related to the legal aspect also. Help them to help you. This is to avoid any confusion which may lead to disqualification of the bid as in many cases purchasers and even users are not so technically informed. One may get the help of a tenderer for some minor deficiencies but to remember that the offer may be rejected on one issue without keeping any option to rethink. The technical bid should be absolutely free of any price information or hint, not in number or letter or any other way, neither in price schedule nor in the quotation related to other parts which are the percentage of price like AMC/CMC/clearing/discount/buyback offer etc.

Sometimes it creates a confusion about whether EMD should be attached with tech or price bid if it is not clear in the tender document. Because EMD can indicate price sometimes when asked as a percentage of the quoted price. I suggest, keeping it in a separate envelope, sealing the envelope with the clear marking of tender reference. Enclose the envelope with tech or price bid whatever instructed. If no instructions are given then enclose it with the tech bid. Never send it unsealed or inside the price bid.

Last but not the least, the entire documents should be bound properly (preferably spiral binding so that no page can be altered) with serial number marking on each page. Many of you must have witnessed that the volume of a bid is sometimes more than a thousand pages. In case of such a big tender insert separator sheets for each section for absolute clarity.

The uniqueness of the subcontinent is that many bids get cancelled because of some trivial mistakes. Although in such cases the purchaser is supposed to seek documents and/or clarification. However, the wrong phase 'customer is always right' sets the course in this subcontinent. So, it is better to be perfect & proactive rather than challenging the purchaser later.

5. **Special situations** – though I called this a special situation but this is quite common when dealing with high-value products.

In general, higher-quality products have higher level of specification and are more expensive than lower quality products. So, selling a good product is always challenging in a price-sensitive market, especially where it has to pass through a rigorous and outdated tender process in which the seller has less control.

Points 1 & 2 mentioned above play a vital role in it. But that is not all. One has to be an expert on the rules & regulations of the tender process. Sometimes it is beyond the information available in tender documents. Panoramic knowledge and information can only help in this situation.

It is required to lock the specification if the seller wants to sell the best product while retaining the desired margin. Needless to mention that selling without proper margin can be counterproductive. Walkout can be a better option sometimes. But one need not walk out if he/she understands the process and lets the purchaser realize the same. There are provisions of selling in single-bid with lock-in specification in the first tendering itself to avoid conflict situations. My team sold more than half of the high-value products ranging from fifty lakh (80k$) to five crores (800k$) in single bids after locking the specification. We could convince the customer that there were no alternatives to getting the best products while having the present system that supports them. One can go through 'CSIR manual for best practices', which is followed as a base by other agencies, to strengthen his/her knowledge and confidence.

When I wrote this article there was no eTender or GeM. However, most of the fundamentals are same, only the form changes in eTender. GeM is completely a different process and evolving fast. GeM is not mature enough still to handle the Lifescience business. One needs to study GeM separately. As well as 'Make in India' is becoming most important. One to follow the government notification of it issued time to time. This is not fundamental but like one of the vital requirements of the product. So, no separate discussion is required as this article is on processes mostly.

As I stated before, this is not following any textbook guideline but tailor-made guidance based on my experience in selling with high success as a sales representative at regional/ national level manager. The purpose is to provide some insight into it and provoke thought.

CUSTOMER SATISFACTION

Art of Trapeze with Science of PID

Human beings are the only living creature in the universe who can smile. The smile comes with satisfaction. Our business territory is in the land of Lord Buddha who was born here and conquered the world's heart with his elegant & blissful smile. However, it is the most difficult task to create a smile in the face of argumentative Indians. Our friends of neighbouring countries also have the same DNA dashing the political barriers.

However, it is challenging but not that difficult.

Service providers do this challenging task, as they are meant for an entire workforce of an organisation to enjoy the benefit. Service providers means those who are primarily responsible to provide engineering, application, logistic support. At times others also get involved but not as standard practice.

How to win the confidence and satisfaction of a customer, satisfaction itself is a most subjective matter. It does not depend only on the quality, promptness, economy etc. of the services. It depends on how nicely one can measure & manage customers' expectations and maintain delivery levels accordingly. The delivery level has its own threshold and limit as service providers' work under certain limitations. Budget, quality and quantity of manpower, the site at a difficult location etc. are some of the major limitations. Managing a proper inventory is the most tricky and skilful task on this list. Ironically customer satisfaction gets maximum weightage on their performance review, sometimes in paper but always at the back of the mind of all. Spewing of service is not the solution. The success is hidden under the skillset of how one can MEASURE customer's expectation, MANAGE it within the permissible delivery level and BALANCE the delivery in a win-win situation. On the contrary, one can end up giving everything losing one's interest but that may not bring the desired result.

So, one has to be an expert in the balancing act. In my view, the master of all balancing techniques is PID, which can be applied here. I understand the term is new to many of the readers unless one has an electronics engineering background. Let me explain it in brief. PID is widely used in instrumentation as a controlling circuit for balancing moving parts, voltages, light, sound, heating elements etc. precisely, where a transducer provides feedback to input as proportional (P) of output, the input signal is then integrated (I) in a circuit with desired level signal & produces a quick response to output and derivative (D) circuit provide overall (can say slower) response to prevent oscillation or overshoot. In another word one is quick error detection and adjustment, the other is over the time error estimation and set course accordingly. (I would like to name it as 'Short & Quick' and 'Long & Strategic' for convenience of discussion.) Altogether this provides a stable and sustainable balanced result. Just look at it from a different angle with a physical example to simplify. A trapeze walker uses his body for quick balancing and uses a long cross-bar to balance the overall centre of gravity. Both are very important otherwise s/he would not be able to reach the goal and may topple on the way.

As a service support provider one needs to put a proper feedback matrix in place, to measure and control expectations spontaneously as well as overtime and set delivery standards accordingly. Here the most important thing is to find clean feedback so the rest of the processes are accurate.

Short & Quick: Best quick feedback can be achieved by calling important customers' in a planned manner and regular basis. This is the area which is often most neglected. It takes a few minutes only per customer. Each important customer should be contacted at least once a month or at least once in a quarter based on the nature of the business and to take important feedback in an informal way. The best is to meet them and talk, as much as possible. This can help to generate the most trustful information and quick action can be applied. However, this feedback can have errors of profound recent occurrence.

The formal survey can be the second option by sending internet links where customers can provide feedback spending a few minutes. SurveyMonkey kind of sites can be used.

Though this discussion is targeting external customers but it can be used for internal customers also.

Long & Strategic: This should be elaborated and matured. A confidential Survey through external agencies is a good process as some of the customers may feel shy to provide appropriate feedback in the indirect method. It can be done once in a year or twice for extreme service-oriented businesses. However, as external agencies who are not experts of the business are doing it, the proper set of questions as well as a distinctive section for different divisions dealing with the same customer should be designed to avoid mutilated responses which may lead to the wrong conclusion. One can be unhappy with delivery but very happy with the engineering services or fast installation.

Other than these, there are numerous ways to put a matrix to measure the level of satisfaction and adopt a continuous improvement process to deal with this subjective matter. However, instead of discussing more mantras, I would like to use some anecdotes that add life to this article. More like a story and a story touches the heart and takes its place in our minds forever. Also, it is smoother to read it as IN-post after a hectic day or at a precious weekend.

No feedback is silly – The complaint is related to misbehaving of a machine with a female operator. One of the service engineers of a reputed laboratory instrument MNC found it ridiculous when he got a complaint from one of the female operators about misbehaving of the instrument. She was the only female operator and others are male in three shifts of the pathology department of a reputed hospital. She told, 'I feel shy to say this as it sounds too silly but it is a fact. Whenever I open the door, the rotor comes to stationary states as usual so that I can take vials out. However, when I put my hand inside to take the positive or negative vials the rotor starts moving again preventing me from taking the vials out. It happens most of the time with me but it has never happened with other guys'. The engineer ignored it with a smile that the machine has no diversity issue he had ever heard.

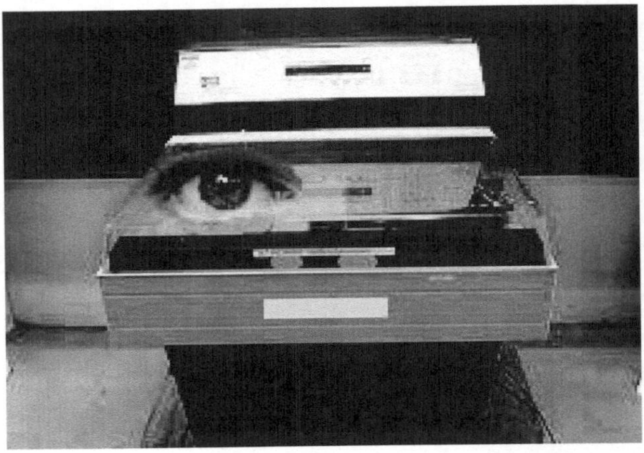

However, as it was really a chronic issue and the gullible operator was desperate to find the solution. One day she called the service manager and stated the fact. The service manager understood the gravity of the matter, discussed with the engineer and thought that some interesting matter should be there which needs better observation and cannot be ignored. So he went to the laboratory with the engineer when the lady operator was on duty. He suggested the engineer to open the door and take out vials several times. He did the same for himself too. Surprisingly the machine did not misbehave with him but the lady intermittently.

Finally, in short, he discovered that the bangle, made of iron and may have some magnetic property, in her right hand triggering the read-relay which passes the signal to the microprocessor whether the door is closed or open. When she puts her hand inside after opening the door, the read-relay triggers once more, signalling the processor that the door is closed and the rotor starts moving.

He suggested that the operator operate with her left hand and resolve the issue once and for all. Not silly but science!

Subjective – It was surprising to all when a customer satisfaction survey among car users revealed that the expected best manufacturer & service provider scored low while a relatively dull one scored highest. It was a concern too for the organisation that conducted the survey. So before they release the risky report, they dove deep into a few opinion reports and found surprising results which helped them to improve the quality of their report and suggestions.

One user of the lower segment stated that he had a problem with starting of his car within a couple of weeks after buying his new car. He had to turn the key twice or thrice to start. So, after observing this for a few days, he called the service station of the manufacturer. They suggested bringing the car to their centre. He drove it to the service station and they rectified the problem within a few hours of his waiting. So he was happy and had given very high marks.

Too expensive, top of the models premier brand user commented adversely for some kind of issue. He had to turn the key twice one day only after 9 months of purchasing the car. On his one phone call, the company sent a technician to the parking lot in his office. The technician checked, did something and assured him that he would not have the same issue again. It never happened again. But he is unhappy because such a premier & expensive car should not have such problems even for once within several years of purchase. So he has given low marks to give the proper message to the company.

I feel the message is clear to all of us.

Passion – Story of a car salesman. He sold the highest number of cars as an individual for more than two decades doing the same job and placing his name in the Guinness book of records. He was an employee of the director level but liked to stand at the gate of the biggest showroom of Chevrolet. He was inviting customers from there, convincing and selling the car with equal passion. But the interesting & unique thing is that the customers were getting a handwritten letter within a few days of purchasing the car from his daughter which says 'thank you for purchasing a car from my daddy'. Also, he was arranging get-togethers of his all customers a regular intervals to get candid feedback and suggestions.

People think that he used to write the letters himself in the name of his daughter. However, it does not matter much when it pleases someone and says 'we care'. The name of the salesman is Joe Girard who won almost all records as a salesman in the automobile industry. An ideal example of passion, developing relations and getting feedback to deliver satisfaction.

It is not important how much we believe or do not believe these stories. But all these stories have some underlining message which can help service providers to deal with the customers in a smarter way. Good quality products can attract customers but quality support will make it drool-worthy and that is what we all look for in this arduous game.

Few lines were encouraging me which I kept in the wall of my cabin when I was regional and later National service manager. Check these below –

If you fail to plan, you are planning to fail.

Indecision is the worst decision.

Service delayed is service denied.

However, all of these are easy to accept, difficult to start and tough to practice. Only, love of own organisation, work and satisfaction of selling smile can make it easy.

THINK DEEP BEFORE THINK BIG

All of you must have gone through several professional trainings. What is the most correct answer in a training course when a trainer asks a question? It is not necessarily most correct but usually, it is the answer that the trainer wants to hear to channelize his/her thought, irrespective of the answer being a blunt one or partly correct. But in case you think differently or beyond boundaries and have a unique innovative mind then you can be stamped as odd.

What dumbfound you were in your first training? You uttered, 'what a great example!' Most probably that is the 'Glass and Water' paradox to prove something. The question is presented like this, an interviewer asks an interviewee, "what do you see" keeping a glass partly filled on the table in front of him.

What is that supposed to prove? Positivity and Negativity. Half glass full means you have a positive mind and half glass empty means you have a negative mind. What a childish conclusion!

In some cases, the trainer goes to the next step like Opportunities..... Content...Satisfied...etc.

In fact, the question or example itself is a little blunt.

Why is this question blunt? Because the expected answer is 'half glass full' or 'half glass empty' to meet the requirement of the next explanations of the trainer. With ignorance of the vast hidden potential of this example. Blunt answer because –

i. How do we know if the water or liquid is 'half'? Superficial! Is it not appropriate to say partly filled or empty?

I feel a better similar question can be what is the basic colour of a Zebra. Is it white with black stripes or black with white strips?

ii. How one can be sure that it is water just by looking it? It can be any liquid. Is it not too simple a conclusion?

The problem of concluding with half a picture is shown above. What do you feel when you see it? Foolish animal! Rapacious dog! Heights of greediness! Blunt to achieve the target without mind! Don't these come to our mind? Surely. See the same picture in full at the bottom of the article and see how it is foolish to conclude with half picture.

Anyway, let's see what can be a better answer to the Half Glass puzzle. Anticipating one has a scientific and analytical mind and does not conclude with half picture.

What can be another answer of depth for 'what you see?'

A. "H2O". Not a very good answer but simple & scientific.

(Scientific Mind)

B. Matching each other, though both are completely different substances (solid and liquid)".

(Perfect Match)

This is very important in everyone's professional life as well as family life. Two person's thoughts, knowledge, habits, culture, attitude and even physical competencies usually never are equal like the Glass or Water. But they are perfect together and stable. Attitude to match each other, not competing but complementing leads to success.

C. "Vessel helps the liquid to be stable. Otherwise, the liquid can go to waste and damage other things."

(Helping Hand, Cooperation, Empathy)

It is important, especially in corporate life, for managers to give protection to employees who have not yet found a stability because of insufficient experience or any other reason but are positive and transparent. With time they can be turned into the most useful employees of the organisation.

D. "All three states of a substance are there. Solid & liquid which we can see. The vapour we cannot see but it is on top. So if we ignore that then it is a matter of time before the glass is empty."

(Unseen challenges, Prediction, Vision)

E. "The liquid takes the shape of the vessel".

(Accommodative, Humble)

F. "Two transparent creations together" or "the transparency which makes both visible".

I like this the most. Simple, Philosophical. As well as when mind can see beauty first.)

Do you agree that these can be answers expected from people who can think in-depth, have an analytical mind as well as can be innovative by nature? Surely you have come across this question but ever these answers flew into your mind. If the answer is yes then it is great. If the answer is no, no issue, it's time to start deep thinking.

One more example comes to my mind which is a better fit in positivity, opportunity cocoon. I just heard it and sharing below.

The manager of a shoe marketing company sent two salesmen to an island for selling shoes. He called them to review the development after a fortnight as per plan. One salesman started shouting, blaming the manager for wanting to spoil his career and posting him in a place where no one wears shoes.

Then the manager called the second salesman. This salesman started crying with joy, "Sir, what a nice assignment. I found here that no one uses shoes. So it is easy to show them the benefits and capture big opportunities almost without much effort and any competition".

Think big is not big! The majority of people can think big; be blissful or baseless. But if thinking big is not blended with thinking deep at the planning stage then disaster cannot be avoided. This is the reason majority of start-ups fail in spite of entrepreneurial start with zeal and big thought. Think deep is not easy as it requires intellect, knowledge, experience and some amount of madness (which is called out of the box thought in the corporate world but most the people talk about it without having it). However, you can cultivate. Put your all sincerity to –

Think deep before think big!

See the Dog is not a fool. We marked him as a fool, greedy etc as concluded in the half picture.

SPECIFICATION

How Much Matters? What Matters?

In designing, buying or selling a product what comes first is the specification. It matters, but how much? Another opinion is that the benefits matter and not the specification. However, in my view, what matters most is the end result (output) and not the specification or benefits. End result may not be a reflection of specification.

How much is one buyer exposed to the end result? Almost set at nought. We realise it after using the products for days and months. Or in some cases, we never realise it but pay a premium for it.

Sellers emphasise the specification as it is the easiest thing a buyer can understand, compare, decide and feel happy about his/her buying decision. So sellers are in the rat race to make it better knowing that it may sometimes not have any relevance to the use.

How can the myth of specifications can be looked at from a different perspective? Let us take some examples.

Rat race:

Megapixel. How much? Three, five, ten, twenty? It has even crossed 100MP in mobile phones.

What is the output? The mobile screen where 3MP is enough. 5MP gives perfect clarity for laptops or in equivalent size print.

One cannot differentiate the quality for higher MP camera pictures. No one takes pictures in a mobile phone for larger than life billboard advertisements.

However, manufacturers are gradually increasing the MP. The reason is that customers understand & compare this parameter only. It is inexpensive also in today's world compared to other things related to picture quality. In a true sense, the picture quality depends mostly on the quality of the lens, shutter speed, image processing technique, quality (not quantity only) of sensors. However, gullible buyers remain in dark in these parameters and are forced to influence by MP. That is the reason we find dull or hazy pictures in several devices though having higher MP than required.

Let's not bring detail in this discussion about the flip side of high MP, like bigger file size occupies more space, is slow and bites more bytes on net transmission etc. Also to accommodate bigger files we need bigger memory and a bigger cost to pay. It's funny but neither we have any option nor we realise it.

The same thing happens with computer processor speed though the architecture and OS influence the performance most. That is the reason we know that in some systems applications run faster and better when the processor clock speed is lower than its competitors. Also how many know it that not the processor version but the generation plays a bigger role. Mostly, people ignore generation and concentrate on versions to find superiority.

Seller shove on new technology:

Let us look into instrumentation. Many companies emphasise on fibre optics for guiding light signals and buyers feel that it is always better. However, unless it is unavoidable or has a very specific advantage, a reflective mirror or prism light path gives a better result as fibre optics reduce the signal strength substantially where reflective loss is almost nil. We need to look into sensitivity, resolution, minimal detection capacity etc. than whether it is through fibre optics or not.

Bringing negative into positive:

Sometimes companies state that their products are free from detector voltage settings and sensitivity settings etc. When it is in their low priced models, it is invariably to reduce cost and not a beneficial feature. However, ironically we find that these are highlighted in the user's desire list due to ignorance or with some illicit purpose.

Built quality - long term:

Flow-cell, cuvette and capillary are very common components of analytical instruments. The optical specification claimed by the manufacturer is in brand new condition. However, the quality of these components widely varies with the quality of the materials used such as glass, quartz or fibre. So, the specification of a glass capillary can be sometimes better than quartz initially but goes down within a short period through use and clean process, resulting in frequent expensive replacement of these components to pass the quality control/ calibration.

So it is more important to understand what kind of material is used than what is written in the specification sheet. But specification data sheet usually does not carry detail of it. So we need to look into the ultimate output in short term and long term from different sources.

Theoretical superiority:

Several Cell sorters claim a throughput of 20 million cells per second. It is a theoretical speed. No one can achieve it considering other factors as well as no publication available where even half of the speed could be achieved. However, the manufacturer kept the specification to take advantage of the rat race. They use twisted language on purity which is most important. So we need to find what the desired speed is and what purity in that range is and then look at the spec sheet for maximum. Publications and blogs can help a lot in the selection process, not what companies are claiming.

Confuse if can't convince:

Also, there are tricks of setting specifications on the manufacturer's own terms which is beneficial for their product or technology which makes it difficult for the buyer to compare. A lot of contradictory expert opinions float on the net on these making it more complex and confusing.

Clever Specification:

One more interesting matter behind claiming the specification is unknown to many. Some of the manufacturers use the average and some others use the least one.

For example 100 nos. of the instrument is used for beta testing. The purpose is to find the accuracy of an analytical instrument. The minimal and maximum results are 0.2% and 0.9%. The average of 100 results is say 0.4%. Some of the manufacturers would claim the sensitivity as 0.4%. That does not guarantee that the instrument bought by a user gives an accuracy 0.4% or better. It can be less or poorer. Alternatively, some good manufacturers claim accuracy as 0.9% for the same set of test results. That means any instrument out of the shelf should give better accuracy and at least 0.9%, always.

I have chosen one example on each of the topics to limit the contents. However, needless to mention that numerous examples that are there and you may find those giving a deep thought.

So, the thumb rule is to see the end result:

How much the product is solving the purpose?

Quality of result. If you can't see any difference, then it's not higher quality whatever the specification says.

Quality vis a vis cost, value for money

Long term output. Rugged, durable, stable whatever you name it.

It can be available from sellers by deep probing. However, it is best to google it and find out from users across the globe.

ALL EMPLOYEES ARE NOT VALUABLE ASSETS, ARE YOU ONE?

Most of us forming the working class are the employees of different organizations. Many of us indubitably like to hear the phrase – "Employees are the best assets of a company". Hearing this phrase not only gives us pleasure but also instils confidence and sometimes arrogance in us; in fact, a narcissistic employee may feel immensely satisfied on hearing such words.

It is true that employees are supposed to be valuable assets of any organization, however, it is not an unconditional statement. It must be noted that our world as a whole was built on the basis of a variety of factors and conditions, including various physical, chemical, biological and organism-centric factors. Einstein's Theory of Relativity, the success or failure of a movie, our relationship with our friends, family or peers

and the terms of our employees are based upon several conditions and variables. Same for the employees.

No thumb rule can be made and applied for dealing with people. Each one of us is unique in nature. However, each one of us likes to believe that it is important to trust our fellow humans. We will nonetheless find untrustworthy people around us. Similarly, every employee likes to believe that he/she is a performer, irrespective of whether he/she is actually a performer or a non-performer.

One must also remember that the world is a beautiful place to live in only because it still has a number of trustworthy, kind-hearted and well-performing people almost everywhere. Many of such people help the weak or non-performing people around them perform unless the latter do not want to be helped or do not want to perform. The management of any company chalks down its goals and objectives; however, it is the performers who execute the plans leading to these goals, in turn, earning every dollar for the company. Thus, instead of basking in the false glory of being part of a group labelled as a company's asset, one must periodically evaluate oneself and identify one's strengths and weaknesses so that the relevant steps for one's self-development and for upgrading oneself may be taken as and when required.

One of the means for any under-achiever to upgrade himself or herself could be seeking professional and personal help from the achievers around him or her, leaving his/her ego. However, it has been observed that most people either find it difficult to trust their peers and colleagues or are scared of taking their candid opinions, advice or suggestions. In other words, most people do not take criticism in their stride.

Let us take a look at what successful people around the world have stated about an employee. Their words might help us gain insight into this topic and also help us redefine an asset, its importance and useful.

A few years ago, the renowned self-help book writer and keynote speaker Mr Shiv Khera, was invited to attend our company's annual conference as a guest speaker. Just before Mr Khera's speech, the then HR director concluded his speech with the following statement: "Every employee present here is an asset to the company". Upon hearing this, all the employees present in the hall burst with joy. However, Mr Khera caught this statement, broached the subject at the beginning of his talk and asked the audience, "How many of you believe that employees are an asset to a company?" Every employee raised his/her hand to confirm their belief in the statement. Mr Khera, however, retorted saying that this statement is untrue. He further explained that only engaged employees could be an asset to a company and disengaged employees would always be a liability. Although his statement might not have been digested easily by many confreres present in the audience, however, he did manage to convey a simple message with conviction.

A few more comments are captured below. Though most of you might have come across these statements in social media repeatedly. Nice message, encapsulated thousands of pages in a few words about employees which can encourage one to establish her/him be an asset in the career path. I am taking advantage of the belief that repetition is the mother of learning and reprinting below.

Bill Gates was asked in an interview what he did which made Microsoft so great. He humbly replied that he almost did nothing very special. He neither understands software nor hardware or sales much. On repeated requests, he stated that he did only one thing and probably did it the right way. He picked not the best but the right people and put them in the right place. He always did it the right way he believed and the rest is the result. One may find the same statement from him in brief in his famous interview 'The Road to Success' with Warren Buffett as below.

Bill says, "his best decisions had to do with picking the right people to work with. Having somebody who you totally trust, who's totally committed, who shares your vision and yet has a little bit different set of skills, and also acts as a check on you... Some of the ideas you come up with you run by them because you know they're going to say, Hey, wait a minute, have you thought about this and that?"

Jack Ma, the founder of Alibaba Group, created a multi billion organisation in a short period, the first mainland Chinese entrepreneur to appear on the cover of Forbes and the richest person in China follows it and suggested, 'do not hire the most qualified, hire the craziest'. He himself is one of the craziest entrepreneurs, and has been proving it repeatedly.

Once Rushi Modi commented that I never look at fancy matters like qualification, age, gender and race etc but put maximum weightage on creativity. He said, 'not I, but those creative people made TISCO the best performing organisation for decades.

Jack Welch, imparted an organizational behaviour called "boundarylessness". A man behind one of the greatest organizational successes in history (GE) expressed his belief that "getting the right people in the right jobs is a lot more important than developing a strategy."

Last but not the least, by Steve Jobs, "it doesn't make sense to hire smart people and tell them what to do; we hire smart people so they can tell us what to do."

I feel these few examples are good enough to acknowledge how important employees are for the organization. On the contrary, it is not a rare incidence that many organisations lose their most valuable intangible assets because of immature leadership, but that is not the topic of this discussion.

Undoubtedly, skilled and engaged employees are the most valuable assets for the company. In my view when we judge PEOPLE to bring in the boat, we need to focus on a few must-have qualities first like,

P-olite,

E-thical,

O-rganised,

P-erformer,

L-iberal,

E-fficient.

However, if the first two are present then only judge the rest.

Contrast & Bandwidth in The workplace

The source of satisfaction

One of my good friends came and stated that what I have been doing is useless. Is there any fun in our job or are we just a tool to earn?

The friend ironically is in the same type of job for the last two decades. We both joined together as engineers. Later we managed many portfolios like service management, sales & marketing and long time in leadership positions.

That he is telling today is not new but as naysayers, he has been cursing destiny too altogether. I tried to convince him several times that we have huge contrast in our job. As long as the contrast is in life, being personal or professional, it is enjoyable and not boring. We are fortunate that we got some rare opportunities to use our talent while many in my contacts are not that fortunate.

It does matter, how we see ourselves and the world.

If we see the pain we find plenty. Like, we had to travel a lot even with no contact with family for weeks. We were queued in a telephone booth, late-night every day, for a few minutes of conversation with our family. We had to spare chicken in our dinner to manage the expensive STD calls then. But that is Lilliputian compared to the bandwidth of our work & joy. We are fortunate to have been globe-trotting repeatedly and for decades. We were fortunate to travel to many of the world's most exotic places to attend several business meetings.

Sometimes, I get surprised at the contrast in our job which we have been pursuing. However, his statement helped me recollect some memories. I told him, let us go for lunch and recheck our dossier together, which went as below.

Above and below the surface:

It started with the Bokaro steel plant and later in many other places. We were engaged in installing pollution and weather monitoring systems of Thermo-Electron Co. (TECO), USA and William Lambrecht GmbH, Germany in all steel plants. We had to climb on the mast which gives the feeling of touching the sky. It was not required for me to climb as the technicians were supposed to climb but I did not want to miss the rare opportunity.

Also, I did not miss the opportunity to work 50 feet below the water surface in the open sea. This is for the installation of the Torsion meter of Maihak GmbH, Germany in a big ship commissioned by Garden Reach Shipbuilders and Mazagon Doc shipbuilders.

Safest and Wildest:

I have seen how doctors perform corneal transplants in a high-tech operation theatre during the installation of operating microscopes and other instruments. Cool, calm and safe.

I have experienced the other world. I had to walk for miles with a big team through a deep forest of the northeast to install Gallagher Inc. made fence (high voltage cable boundaries between dense forest and nearby habitats) to keep the local inhabitants safe from the wild elephants and cheetahs.

Minute and Mega:

I have worked with the ultra-micro balance where a tiny voltage variation of one microvolt in a load cell can destroy your hours and days long hard work of bringing stability.

On the contrary, I worked confidently with voltage which is one billion times higher than that. As a reference, so-called high-tension lines which deliver power to cities is usually run with the potential of 15/20KV. However, I have the experience of working with 450KV Seifert Industrial X-Ray. A single mistake in putting silicon grease insulation or a trace level of moisture in it can result in a spark pass-through the room killing the operator/engineer and can destroy everything.

Fare – three times:

I cannot forget the days we were travelling from Dhanbad to Bokharo. We, the company representatives were paying three times to occupy three seats in the local trekker or ambassador car. This was not for getting a comfortable seat. Six people were still in the same row virtually ossifying each of us. This was to avoid someone or some big baggage from sitting on the back of our heads or below our knees.

Also, the unforgettable experience of travelling Europe by executive class paying three times the normal fare, lakhs of additions rupee for a few hours more comfort.

Save and break:

I have served the country's defence with the highest level of security and confidentiality by the installation of an Aerial survey system in defence aeroplanes. I felt proud to be a part of an important mission. Also, I spent weeks in an Indian Navy ship during sea trials. I served the navy who serve and save us.

I also came under terror attack and observed terror retaliation from stone throwing distance.

Once I was working to serve AIDS patients in Care Foundation, Manipur; suddenly I saw terrified office staff and doctors shutting doors and running to find a safe corner inside the office. They just pulled me too. We were waiting between life and death with shivers running down my spine. We were startled hearing doors and grills being broken by them one after another. It went on for about 5 minutes but seemed longer than 5 hours. Fortunately, a military convoy which was passing that way saved us. Later I understood that they had come to loot the drugs which are judiciously used to treat the addicted people to avoid the saviour withdrawal effect as a part of treatment.

In another incident about a year and a half ago, when Kashmir was under the highest terror attack of this century, I had to go to Srinagar for a big order closing and got stuck there. On one Friday afternoon when all doctors and staff went to perform Namaz, I was just roaming around SKIMS. In front of my eyes suddenly two militants had come on a motorcycle and opened fire on a military camp. In retaliation one of them was gunned down and the other disappeared. Rest is a different story and not to elaborate here but sometime later in another platform.

Worst order and best gift ever:

The most bitter experience was enjoying the cool environment in the highly decorated large chamber of a medical superintendent in a super speciality hospital, hearing him instruct a group of doctors to increase the sample load of a new machine so that they achieve the target and recover investment fast. Sad!

On the contrary, one day I went to the pathology lab of a hospital and, saw a middle-aged man waiting for me. The technician told me that he came to thank me as he came to know from the doctor that his daughter had been cured because of a timely diagnosis of blood cancer and the credit partly goes to my out of the way support. The first and last time I accepted a gift from anyone related to my profession, a box of sweets.

Sweet and sour experiences never make a journey dreary. The idea is to keep the journey continuing and find beautiful challenges in technical, leadership or business front every day. That is good enough to enjoy our work.

Lunch over, my friend's silence speaks volumes and shows that he has started recollecting equally exciting experiences from the treasure box of his memories. Many of those might have been covered by the cinder of work stress. I am sure, next time he will describe how exciting his work is and not a money vending machine.

I feel this excites you too! Surely you have many such memories to enjoy and thank god, dive deep in your memory and feel good.

Are we ATT.. fit?

While 99% of our genes are the same as the genes of monkeys, what is it that makes us so different? Even different people from the same socioeconomic atmosphere move through a different gradient in their paths and attain different heights of success. WHY?

Genes are made of four elements with a vast combination of ATCG, here we do not want to peep into that complicated science but simplified behavioural elements of social science in fun mood. Just remember ATT and follow it. The words starting with ATT is the differentiator, one day clicked in my mind as I have a habit to play with the resonance of words and sentence. Take it lightly, as learning comes through joy and not by compulsion.

ATTire

The human being is the only species that uses attire. Irrespective of fundamental qualities, perfect attire helps to earn the desired respect from others. Why not, as having a perfect dress sense shows the taste and quality of a person. It is wrong that it requires more money to have a perfect dress but there is another way around it. It does not come through money but intellect. Few thumb rules are,

Need to know what is perfect in which situation. Attending a party in dark trousers and a formal white shirt may indicate a lack of dress sense while the same may score high in the office environment.

Should be sober. We use to communicate face to face with other people round the clock but one face should feel comfortable to communicate with the other. This is the benchmark.

Covering or exposure of the body as per the place, programme, or position. But neither burka nor topless can be sober in any situation (can be arguable).

ATTendance

Be it in the office or social gathering one should be highly punctual. Punctual does not mean on time but in time to ensure other dignitaries don't have to wait.

Attendance is not a presence but giving respect to others by patiently hearing, learning, participating and fulfilling the purpose of attending an event. Mental attendance is more important for our own benefit while physical attendance may be important for others.

ATTention

It is important to hail the attention of others in a refined way. Some people without the inherent quality to seek attention usually try mockery which is always counterproductive.

Also, it is important to give attention to other's requests, instructions, demands or needs as a habitual punctilious.

Besides this it is important to give attention to our own legitimate needs, be it for peace, pleasure or self-development.

ATTached

Are you mentally and physically attached or engaged to your work, with your family and society? One needs to be; to enjoy her/his personal and professional life.

If we take the example of workplace engagement, research says 16% of employees are engaged, 69% are not engaged and 15% are actively disengaged. Only engaged employees deliver the best and grow in any organisation. It can be true in our personal life to lead a peaceful life for ourselves and the people around us.

ATTitude

There isn't much to speak about attitude. It is an unassailable fact that attitude plays not only a big role but is the bandmaster of creating life's symphony, be it in the profession or personal affairs. Experience, qualification and knowledge can fuel a positive attitude and on contrary can also nullify all hard-earned qualities. Attitude only makes a person curmudgeon or wise.

To simplify keep three letters in mind...ATT....

I am not a so-called ATTractive motivational trainer so you have every right to discount my view. However, do you feel that it is easy with ATT denotation to remember and practice these most important life designing factors?

Assorted Thoughts

Capturing a few assorted thoughts which can work silently to give a positive impact, especially to the people stepping into the corporate world. As well as help to cultivate to think differently.

How Long is One Second?

Length of 'one second'. How does it matter? Ek second pe naa train chut jata; yaa sensex gir jata (neither you miss a train in one-second delay nor will the share market crash).

However, can you realize how loooong is one second !!!

In my teenage, when I was an active sportsman and was participating in different events, the world record of 100 metres sprint was approx. 11seconds. It was not that we were taking one minute to run 100 metres. Our timing in the local club was also around 12 seconds. Just 1 second more only to touch the world record!!! Wow!! Can you imagine that there are always more than a billion sprinters around the globe standing within the next one second of the world record? And all of them were practising hours daily round the years but could not manage to reduce the big time of one second.

I was thinking, then, it is just one second...so why not I jump in last moment to cover it.

But in practice, I found that when you have given everything, you are not left with the option or energy to jump. Such a shortcut is easy to suggest but impractical in reality.

Also, it is not one second. It is still more than ten metres to cross with no time left. In the same way, when crossing 100 metre in 10.5 seconds is impossible for millions, it can be a cakewalk for Usain Bolt (now the time is reduced to 9.x second). If performance is raised to a higher level the tough things also become easier.

This is the reason Carl Lewis, Johnson, Usain Bolt are so regarded as they could able to manage just 1/100 of a second from the trailer each and every time. And this 1/100 seconds brings fame and billion dollars. For the same reason, one cannot stay in this top position for a long time. Consistency matters but not easy.

The third part of this thought is that I find the same thing happens in our daily life. If someone is not so intelligent or has less capability compared to his seniors in office, family or society they always come under criticism. However, it may be that one day he/she can outperform the people who are criticizing or attacking him/ her. The difference is sometimes just a fraction of a second which keeps on being broken by juniors with the push of able seniors and not pullers.

Small Talks

You may have come across big-talks and been bored of them. Now you think what is right, these Big Talks or my Small Talks

Big- Never give up!

Small- Why? Better to give up after some try. Never drag too much. Look for alternatives that can be more fruitful. Do not get stuck, go ahead.

Big- You can get anything if you have a strong desire!

Small- majority of desires never get fulfilled is the fact. Capability and execution are important otherwise only strong desire cannot help. Also, desire needs to be practical.

Big- Nothing is impossible!

Small- OMG!. Almost everything is impossible. Things little out of reach only can be possible, not far reach. It is true that many so called impossible things can be made possible with good efforts but the word 'nothing' is part of immaturity or exaggeration.

Big - Be positive always!

Small – Talking positivity has become a fashion. But be practical-positive is important. Only showing positivity does not work. Practising positivity is important. Also, I have noticed that always being positive is a deficiency of deep-thinking ability or avoiding doing much by accepting something someone suggested.

Big- Do it now!

Small- Now? Yes, but not everything. Time heals and time builds. Everything has its own time. Some matters only can be 'right now'. Though do not defer unless you find right now is not the right time to do it. Do not make deferring a habit.

Be Honest Before You Are A Religious Person.

Do you have a belief on God??

If the answer is yes then go ahead. Otherwise, stop reading.

Do you feel God is a fool?

Does God believe in what you talk and pray?

Does God answer your prayers accordingly?

Do you think God does not know all about your bad work, wrong deed and good work? Think.

Do you feel God is greedy?

If God is a superpower, infinite, made everything, and can destroy everything as per your belief then how is it possible that he/she may be pleased by the amount of Peda or Gold you put on god's feet?

Do you feel that poor people get less blessing because they just fold hands and pray, compared to the people earning in a wrong manner in business or in job and offering more? How foolish!

Give something reasonable to show faith and love, like what we usually do when visiting our relatives/neighbours houses.

Do you feel God is jealous?

It is beyond question and already resolved unanimously that God can be one energy. One and only one.

(Cannot be as we think the multiple in Hinduism, Allah or Jesus or any other forms. These imaginations are to concentrate our minds to cultivate good practices.)???

Do you feel God loves revenge?

They have beaten our guy so kill one of theirs. Is this what God wants? No explanation is required.

Do you feel God need your help to survive?

Many people think so? And feel proud to think so. It is insulting to God.

Do you feel God is illiterate?

Why do we worship in such languages which we do not understand well? Like Sanskrit, Urdu etc. God surely know your language also so pray simply. Though the impact of typical languages and verses is very pleasant at times, but it is not mandatory to pray in these languages. We can surely pray in Hindi, Bangla, Tamil, English or any of our own languages. Pay priest something as it is his (no her. Why ?) profession. But please do not get fooled!

Try! The result will be the same as it will not depend on what you ask but what is your will.

Do you feel God is your friend?

Try and see the result. The abandoned peace in your mind.

I know people avoid any discussion on God. They show they love God but in fact are afraid of God as if God is a villain. They even do not realise it.

If you are afraid then think this way that you are saving God from being hijacked by dirty religious businesses (political or religious) who in fact do not have any belief in God, just make and use religious typical beliefs for their own benefits.

Do good…keep some faith…that's all. You need not do propaganda to support god. God is big enough…strong enough to do what is right. You try to do right for other people besides you and not necessarily for God. Honesty and good deeds are the best way to serve God.

Honesty is not a quality but a primary necessity. Though organisations coach the employees in this direction but I believe it is mostly in the blood, comes from the family. And it is simple…I am honest, that's all.

Pleasure is ultimate

We do not realise the depth....that is; we live for pleasures. Everything we do ultimately for this. Pleasure brings peace.

What can give us real pleasures? 10 happiness tips.

1. Help, help, help...one cannot change the world but can change some people's lives.

2. Be first to resolve conflict and ego issues. Never expect both should equally forward. Extend your humbleness and it will be a magic diluter.

3. If you helped ungrateful persons the best opportunity is to repeat it. Let them realise by themselves and you cannot change

them by advice. Because they are not you. But one day...keep hope.

4. Everything has something positive. Build a passion to see that. The future world will be for positive people to prosper. Nothing else.

5. There are always a few reasons at least for everyone to remain happy. Focus on those. Life is short. Every day passes is shortening your life by one day.

6. Some big and small troubles are inbuilt in everyone's life. Pass them holding your emotions and finding solutions in a content manner. You cannot solve problems ahead of time. Here some faith and attitude is required to make solutions work.

7. Everyone feels I am doing right and others are wrong. Tell yourself 'Just shut up!'. No one is great, no one is absolutely bad. It is our foolishness of feeling superior. Your counterpart also feeling the same.

8. There are always some people who apparently look better or poorer than you. Just ignore and see how fortunate you are.

9. Be honest! No, if and buts. Just be honest always in any situation with anyone as much as possible. Achieving absolute level may be imagination only for anything, so the bottom line is I shall not be dishonest for my own benefit as well as as much can be avoided even for that I need to sacrifice something.

10. Nothing better than the feeling 'I'm good'.

We know all these things. We know yoga is best for health. We know how to swim. However, knowing does not help but practice. These 10 happiness fundamentals are the toughest to practice and easiest if one can imbibe. Once you are happy, you can make others happy and you can contribute best in your profession and for society.

Survival Challenge

You must have read this story I found somewhere. "Every morning in Africa, a gazelle wakes up, it knows it must outrun the fastest lion or it will be killed. Every morning in Africa, a lion wakes up, it knows it must run faster than the slowest gazelle, or it will starve. It doesn't matter whether you're the lion or a gazelle - when the sun comes up, you'd better be running."

Running fast is important.

Technology - Stuck At Last-Century

You must be overwhelmed finding the massive boom of technology and innovation. However, hardly any major unique things have been invented in the last 25 years on electronics & technology...except two things.

You may be thinking that I am mad. Technology is booming in the last few decades and I am telling almost nothing unique. Yes, for a common man it is a utility boom but not an innovation boom. The innovation boom happened mostly in 80s and partly early 90s of the last century. You just name it and all were there at that time.

Let me explain as a technologist and a guy who is passionate about electronics.

Recall 486/Pentium chips and related computers. A breakthrough in the early 90s. After that nothing was unique, only speed changed and size reduced. Pentium to i7 it's the same story. More memory, more speed and less space. Are you thinking of CDs?. It was also invented in 80s but became available for the common man in 90s.

Hard disk became slimmer with SSI replacing HDD. It is again a size reduction and speed escalation. Non-volatile RAM was invented in the late 80s. It was a global big news, invented in Germany and I was fortunately there at that time.

So, laptop computers have taken place of desktops and become slimmer and slimmer. Its development and not a unique invention.

The Internet came in 80s and became popular mostly for email in 90s. Again the speed only increased and some development but not invention.

Then what are the two things which I am saying are unique inventions?

1. GPS

It really changed the world. It is not only Google-Map but the majority of apps, entire eCommerce and trillions of dollars data-sharing revenue of Google and others are based on this location identifier. How it works...very simple but unique, based on some simple mathematical calculation with the help of geo-satellites. Not enough scope here to discuss but interested people can study further.

2. Cloud technology.

Remember those days, even 10/15 years before most of the computer was running based on software those were installed in the hard disk itself.

Then the cloud technology arrived. One did need not to install gigabytes of data in the hard disk. Rather a fraction of it, say few megabytes and that small software knows how to pull the required software and data from the cloud and how to send back/store the data in the cloud. This means you have a key only and can enter any car, drive it and leave it anywhere keeping the key with you. And the entire development of mobile phone apps is just because of cloud technology.

Today's business world, as well as the services, are almost cent per cent based on apps and it is possible only because of the unique development of GPS and CLOUD technologies in the last one decade.

One may say, the smartphone is a unique development. But what is unique in it? The touch screen we were using in the early 90s in some of the high-end instruments. Steve Jobs, the real great thinker used it nicely in the Mobile phone. Mobile phone technology also came in the early 90s. Yes, digitalisation played a vital role besides location, touch etc making the mobile phone so popular.

One more big development is forthcoming. As not yet popular among the common man, I did not mark it as 3rd. It is Metaverse. Study it to know more to update yourselves.

CV-WHAT IS RIGHT?

I have come across many suggestions about the proper way of writing a CV. Let me put my two cents as a key recruiter who handles dozens of CV every week and recruited hundreds of employees for white-collar jobs. .

I learnt that usually, a recruiter spends 60 seconds checking a CV for it to qualify. Is it? Probably not! I get a few dozens of CVs every week through our HR. Honesty, I spend 20 sec or less to qualify. If qualified, then, of course, I spend a good time on it.

What I try to find in a CV primarily are – location (present address), experiences & qualifications. The rest of the things do not come in effect to qualify. Surprisingly complete address is missing in a large number of CVs or it is difficult to trace the location of the present job.

So I suggest you asseverate as below-

1. Put your name and present **ADDRESS** on top. If your name spelling is confusing like my name, mention male/female. Because different job types or locations sometimes demand it.

2. Write clearly about what **kind of job** you are looking for. Also if you are looking for a job in any specific location. Do not expect the recruiter to be enthralled after reading your career objectives which everyone writes well in google age. Also, big common talks (nocebo), like 'looking for a challenging...' does not make any sense. Your CV itself says who you are.

3. Then write about your **EXPERIENCES**, the latest on top. Better to write your achievements/millstones you achieved along with product detail and customer segment; especially if applying for a Sales & Marketing job.

4. **QUALIFICATION**, highest on top with the year of passing for all.

5. **CTC** - most immaterial part in CV. Your present remuneration can be less or more than your market value. Leave it for the next level.

6. **1/2 PAGES Only** - CVs can be one page or max two. Recruiters are intelligent enough to find the fitment and can explore more during interviews. For PhD applicants it can be one page more to showcase publications in brief. However, the CV should not itself thick like a publication

7. **Photo** - I feel putting a decent picture can be preferably pp size, is good. But not essential like all above 6 pints.

Try to put all this important information on the first page. Use font size 11 of standard ms-word font with bold headings. Avoid cockade or decoration.

8. Write the 'Subject Line' if send my mail and 'File Name' appropriate. It should be like 'CV-your name-Date' in my view

and not just Resume, updates resume, scan1234, Cv2 etc which shows a person is casual and no one like to recruit a casual person.

You can write the rest of the things but try to limit it in two pages. The interviewer can find detail during the interview, even beyond what you can predict.

Though it is my thought but maybe not precisely. A few dozen of my close friends are national business/operation/HR heads in large Indian organisations or in multinationals and in close interaction they also share almost the same opinion.

Do not expect to get a reply. If your CV qualifies then recruiters are intelligent enough to reach you. However, one gentle reminder by call or mail can work well. If you get a bad response for your one follow-up call; you should feel happy that you saved yourself to work under a curmudgeon. If you always get a good response by calling them repeatedly, then also the organisation may not be smart enough to cut waste of time. Also, you may be too desperate or missing fitment to join in a good work culture....take care.

RESPECT YOUR RESPONSIBILITY

The Tendulkar's way!

It was day one after changing over to a new job, one of my juniors, the senior most in the team, met me and said, '...ultimately we have a good leader and not a boss'. I did not know her well. 'How do you know that I am a leader?' I asked. I got the reply, 'we know, we heard about you that you are not a conventional manager but a leader'.

The first comment encouraged me. Living in ecstasy for a moment, the second one confused me. I always wanted to be a good manager as a primary need, keeping leadership in the process of learning and implementation. Because, I have seen many people are crazy to prove in a superficial way that they are leaders, ignoring their primary responsibilities, the expectation of the organisation from them and the passion required to be a leader. Ultimately they land into a no man's land.

I have noticed that with the abundant socialization, social media has created hype on 'leadership'. With the help of several comments & cartoons, an image has been created that Leaders are heroes and Managers are villains and have made it an adage. So, at random people are trying to portray that s/he is a leader. Abrupt tawdry 'likes' and 'comments' flooded in LinkedIn/FB etc.

What do organisations really want? Organisations that spend several dollars for some purpose and purposes are neither the same nor static. My experience says the majority of companies need good managers to manage the business, to ensure stability and growth. Also at times, organisations need good leadership quality from some of the managers and it is not necessary that every manager be a leader. But managerial competencies of managers cannot be compromised.

I have no intention of defining leader and manager which is available in plenty on the net and in several bestselling books. (I can refer to 'Leadership Challenge' by Kouzers & Posner for a clear understanding of Leadership as the first step.) I wanted to write this article for the cross-section of employees where more clarity is required and not for true leaders.

Let us peep a bit on what conventional definition differentiates L&M and what should be as I believe.

Use most to appeal: L- heart/ M- head.

The proper balance of IQ/EQ is best. But the application of IQ is foremost and EQ makes it better.

Pursue L-Vision / M – objective.

The objective is bread and butter for all. Vision at a certain level is important.

Essence: L-change/ M-stability.

Both are a must. But change needs to apply after ensuring stability.

Desire: L-achievement / M – result.

The result is an uncompromised need. Achievements are sweeter.

Risk: L- takes / M-minimise.

Minimizing risk is essential.

Also some of the comments in social media, I find are cheap and impolite, Leaders give credit and take the blame but managers do the opposite. Leaders motivate and managers order. Leaders lead from the front but managers suggest. One of the most critical criticisms floating in the net is managers light a fire under people and leaders light a fire in people. We are truly living in a world of freedom of speech! Are we not unknowingly playing the role of cyberbully?

Here I am taking the risk to express my opinion instead of joining the bandwagon, you may or may not agree but I know that you will give a second thought to it. Does it sound like I am against 'Leaders'? No! Neither in this article nor in practice. The purpose is to dissect the matter then to say 'all is well'.

One need not pull down something to glorify something else. So, stop complaining and look positive. The comment of great Chinese philosopher Confucius can be an ideal one in this context.

"It is better to light one small candle than to curse the darkness."

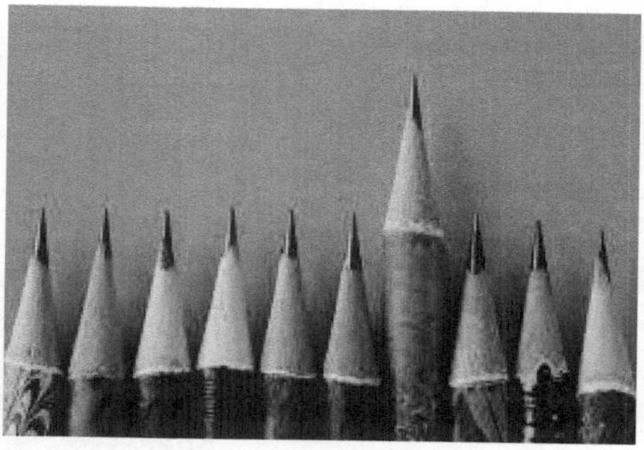

We all can sing, write and paint. However, some of us can only get the wow. Because it requires special skills which can be acquired by learning and experience. This implies in this case too. Though many of us think that leadership is an inherent skill that requires a charismatic style and a loud personality, this is untrue. Also, the myth that leadership is something that one can find/use only in the highest level of organisation or society. The truth is anyone can be a leader. One needs to learn and develop the skills.

Also, there are no conflicts but management and leadership must go hand to hand. One has to complement the other.

I believe the seed of the problem is confusion between Boss and Manager. Certainly bossing means behaving isolated with a lack of vision, empowerment, motivation and all boiled down to get a quick result. So, in the long run it damages the environment, relation and long term benefits of the people and the organisation. So, bossing should be avoided and to learn managerial and leadership skills.

I cannot suppress the temptation of sharing a story that can help to conclude the discussion with the right message.

It was the time when Sachin Tendulkar started playing test cricket. One day Sunil Gavaskar had noticed that Sachin was noting something in his diary in the green room after the day's play was over. Sunil asked him what he was doing. Young Sachin replied that he is noting down how many runs he had scored that day, how many boundaries and over boundaries etc. He also said that he does it sincerely every day during every match. Sunil suggested, he need not to do so and put his all sincerity to develop his skills. If he could play well and score high then there will be thousands of people who would do this job for him. If he fails to play well then his own notes also would have no value for the rest of the world. Sachin followed it and we all know that millions of people started keeping his record. His fandom keeps it on the tip of his tongue.

Look at it from a different angle too. Neither he claims nor do we care about his leadership qualities but he is the highest contributor in the world of cricket. He did what he could do best, what the country (read as an organisation) and cricket (read as an industry) wanted from him. There are several great leaders in cricket but there is no conflict between the greatness of great Sachin and the great leaders.

One has to concentrate her/his focus on developing knowledge, skills and competencies step by step. Be a good manager first and then a leader. Who knows, this way one can walk through his career path being a manager, leader and become a legend too!

THINK REVERSE

if KISS Does Not Look Like A Good Option

If the boat is stuck in the shallow stream, jump over and set the course. Sometimes you need to pull back instead of pushing it to cross the hurdle.

Relax, take it easy. Let us see something in a reverse way. So, fasten your seat belt to sustain some jark I am going to give you.

I am a little bored of hearing; out of the box thinking, leadership, innovation, brainstorming kind of heavy jargons vis a vis let go. But I love KISS. Look around and Keep It Simple & Straightforward. But that does not work always. If one cannot straightforwardly find ways then look upside down.

Let me put some seeds.

Fast forward:

Suppose you are going for a sabbatical leave. You may sometimes get worried about the smooth operation entrusted to you and your team. What you are supposed to do is to distribute your work to subordinates & empower them.

So, make an elaborate list of who has to perform which task. Discuss with your team and let them buy your thought mutually with some correction if needed.

Note that I started the topic with 'suppose'. So, you are not going on leave. In spite of that let the team perform accordingly as if you are not present. Release the monkey from your back. Now you have a better time to carry much higher responsibilities. More time for innovation. Implementation or upgrading strategy, product, process. Your subordinates will have better maturity and encouragement.

Often, people do not get promoted; not because they are not ready for the next level but because subordinates are not ready to take their manager's responsibility.

Push this fast forward button to move forward together.

Hate but get:

Hate terrorists, as much you can. But learn passion from them instead of from a priest.

See, how they sacrifice their life for passion and take all risks. A priest can be faked but not a terrorist. A single mistake in their strategy can blow out his/her life whereas mistakes of priests and other professionals may not be that fatal.

Here I would like to mention, though out of context, that supreme fools only can be converted as terrorists, by deformed ideology. We must hate a terrorist and pity them.

The gist is, as a priest, what looks apparently wise but may not be so always. What looks worst can sometimes teach a good lesson in part if you can filter out the bad part.

Blindfold vs mindful:

We all think lawyers are the ultimate knowledgeable person for legal matters. Whatever they suggest is best. But have you thought that their failure as a whole is 50%, which is very high. When they fight with peers in court, they get exposed that he/she may be wrong or others may have better knowledge. Lawyers are famous for making a faux pas. So, their suggestions may not always be trustworthy.

Equally, better not to follow blindly the theories related to sales/ marketing/relationship as in the textbook, even proven one. Every situation is different and you can be the best person to decide your action as you have the best knowledge of the matter. However one should be strong on fundamentals. Keep the confidence. If one is not confident enough then take the help of someone nearby whom you feel better informed or has better knowledge in the same domain or better IQ to help you.

Reverse the verse:

The efficient process is rhythmic like a verse. However, when the rhythm gets dislocated and cannot bring back the normal process we can look the reverse way.

Easy to understand with some examples.

One manager asked his order processing team how they can make the life of customers' miserable, to list it out.

The responses were something like this –

- We shall work in a reactive manner.
- Work like a solvent.

- Shall not keep records and should not maintain follow-up process.
- Shall not reply to emails/queries prompt.
- Keeping documentation is not important when an order is executed.
- Shall not recheck the price minutely but shall go as in order.
- Month closing is not critical.
- Shall keep reasons ready that it is not my fault but someone else.
- Shall anticipate that the payment term is correct.
- Shall work on it after I finish other works.
- For queries, shall put the ball in other's court and work when the reply comes, not my responsibility anymore.

Then the manager asked the team to reverse all these and that will become an efficient order processing system to achieve high customer satisfaction.

Odd thoughts are not easy to digest but easy to reject. Not necessary that all agree. In spite of that, I am taking the courage to express myself in case some of you find it interesting. At least help you to cultivate a creative thought process.

If the boat is stuck in a shallow stream, jump over. But make sure that you can swim and not only that you know how to swim.

SKILFUL NEGOTIATION

PSN – Professional Selling and Negotiation Skills in brief

Negotiation is the most important learning for Sales and Marketing Professionals. Anyone can be a painter if the outcome would be a black canvas. But when the expectation is wow, then one needs to learn the tricks and acquire the skills. The same is true for negotiation but often people do not focus on it. To make it more damaging, people feel that they can do it well but it is not possible unless people learn the process. They fail to realise their mistakes. As a consequence, the company is ruined, be it a frontline salesperson or top executives. The biggest myth is more experience means can do better negotiations. Understanding the process is most important besides other knowledge.

Let us learn what is the negotiation process, when to start, when to get engaged and when to avoid? What are the skillsets and process of orientation required, etc in a storytelling mood?

Never land into a trap of negotiation unless your selling is complete. One example can make it clear. Suppose a salesperson meets a government customer for selling window air-conditioner machines, the simplest product we all use and easy to understand. The customer selects the model for which the company quotes 50k per unit. Now customer demands 40K. The salesman knows that he can go upto 44K for 20 units. So, he/she skilfully closes it at 45K thinking it is a win-win-win case. The customer was also happy that he could negotiate well. The salesman thought that it is a win for the customer, a win for him and a win for the company. Now let us see, how the company can suffer because the salesman did a premature negotiation before closing the sales process. After price finalisation, they started discussing the supply and installation plan. Then customer opined that the machines need to be supplied in 20 different hospitals across the states. The salesman had to accept it as it is now made or mar for both as the customer has no additional budget. The delivery was mentioned as free without any condition in the offer. When the discussion progressed further it also appeared that the electricity condition in those hospitals are not good so they need stabilisers. The customer here was not demanding much, but politely put his desire to supply one stabiliser with each AC machine. Now salesman has to do it for the safety of the instrument otherwise they may spend more during the warranty period on repeated failure. Also, in some of the hospitals, it may risky to hang it outside without steel framing. I think no more explanation is required about what is the condition of the salesperson now and the case became Win-RUIN-RUIN.

So, negotiation is a process that needs to start after the sales process is over, rechecked, and reconfirmed. A salesperson should understand what is sales process as without this cannot move further to understand the negotiation process. So let us talk that what is selling and sales process?

What is Selling?

Selling is the way that the salesperson helps customers to buy products and services from his/her business. He/she needs to be able to meet the needs of the customer and provide value for money solutions. At times the need may not be visible to customers or they may not have the urge and here salesperson/ organisation need to make needs visible or to create the need.

Basic Responsibilities of a salesperson

The overall responsibility of a salesperson can be explained in 8 stages. These are briefly.

Lead finding - Cold calls/ read shows, mails, website etc.

Funnelling - Qualified suspects and prospects.

Presentation - 101 or/and formal.

Follow-up - Remove bottleneck, keep customers engaged & gain agreement.

Negotiate - If required.

Order - Commercially clean order in hand is important.

Invoicing & Delivery - At this point sale is ensured.

AR collection - Completion of project.

Repeat/ New - Work for the next one.

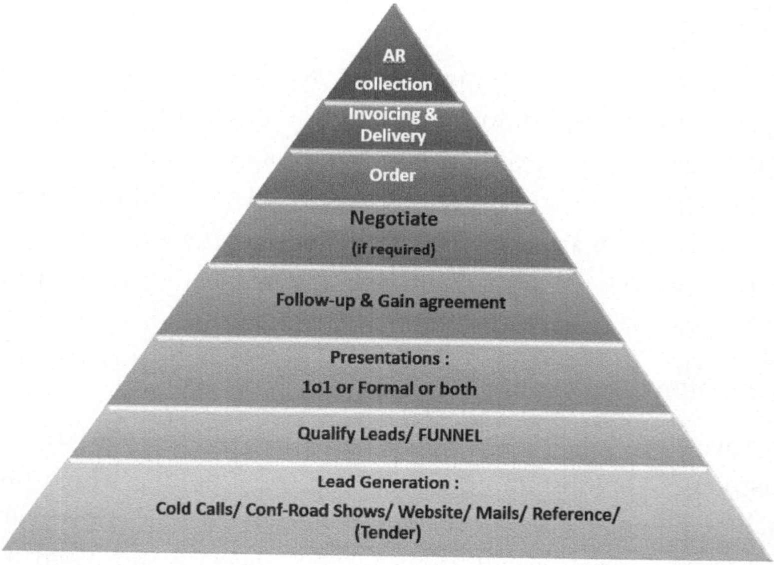

These are my thought on the overall responsibility of a salesperson. It can be more or less depends on the organisation's expectation and the nature of products but overall, these are the vital stages.

As in the above statements, a salesperson work starts by the visiting customer. Following steps can be a good guideline.

Preparations for the customer meeting:

He/she needs to have a good preparation for this. It may be important to fix an appointment and in some cases, a cold call can be ok. We need to understand the customer and take preparation for it. Preparation can be the need of some documents, references, rehearsal of what to say and what can be the counter-arguments etc. Most important is to define the goal. A goal does mean the order or final success, but every meeting should have some purpose as well as a goal to be reached. It can be as simple as making customers agree to a formal presentation.

Meeting :

The next step is meeting. Better to define a timeline and agenda, in the beginning, to make the customer comfortable with clarity. Appropriate probing with a combination of close and open questions is necessary. We need to avoid asking any sensitive information which can jeopardise the entire process. In the end, ask for agreement even if it is a baby step achiever and fix the next meeting/action agenda.

Conditional Agreements:

In this way, a stage will come when the salesperson and the customers come to an agreement on some points, which may include a disagreement on some points. If the salesperson and customer agree on all points then there is no need for negotiation and the lead reaches maturity. However, often it does not happen. So, we need to address the points which are not agreed upon, which means need to negotiate.

Recheck and reconfirm:

However, it is most important to review with the customer jointly with full clarity which are the points both sides agreed on and which are the points disagreed. The best practice is to capture those in a mail or letter and then go for negotiation.

Negotiation- Start Point:

When reconfirmation is over, one needs to start negotiation on the points which are not mutually agreed upon. When we say negotiation, what spontaneously comes to our mind is price negotiation. However, negotiation can mean anything that the two parties disagreed upon. It can be terms and conditions, deliverables, configuration and price. Here, remember not to jump into the price unless deliverable, terms etc can be agreed upon, which you must have seen in the example at the beginning of this article.

Negotiate Deliverables:

Let us see a little more in depth what deliverables can be disagreed upon. It can be the quality of the products, volume/quantity of supply, after-sales services etc.

Negotiate Terms & Conditions:

Terms and conditions can be the Payment term, Legal clauses, return policy etc.

Negotiate Price:

Price is also not simply the currency but anything which costs the sales organisation like the basic price of the products, price of services, rental or outright, other charges, tax etc.

Negotiation – Does and Don'ts:

When one goes into a negotiation, a few things need to kept in mind. These are to create a friendly environment and not that one is trying to twist the arm of other. Understand difficulties or limitations of the other side and if this is not considered, the result can fail to reach a common understanding and the order may be lost. Both sides need to focus on closing and when both sides reach a common agreement the thing one needs to keep in mind is not to discuss anything further as it can spoil a mature case. Keep fooling in mind.

- Establishing a friendly and mutually respectful environment
- Listen first carefully and giving full attention (note vital points)
- Speak with confidence
- Put polite pressure with alternative suggestions
- Make customer to think even his mindset is non-aligned with you
- Concession as possible and remind pride/ quality
- Focus on closing
- Do not linger once deal is closed

Negotiation Key Factors:

Timing

As I stated above, to check and recheck that the sales process is completed. Do both parties have agreement and disagreement

with full clarity. If the answers are 'yes', only then it is the right time to negotiate.

Insight

Who are the people in the negotiation meeting? Who is/are KOLs? What is their mindset and style of negotiation? How flexible or rigid they are?

Strategy

First recapture the differences and agree again. Instead of one solution for each issue, give alternatives. Define minimally acceptable things and what maximum can be achieved.

Final Point of Negotiation- negotiation Styles:

Now come to the most critical points which can make the deal win-win-win. That is, what are the different styles of negotiation. It can be that one style that works better in one case and other styles for other cases.

Make concession - Accept what the customer asking if it is permitted. The advantage is, it helps to close the case fast. Sometimes it may so happen that after a long negotiation the salesperson may need to give more than this.

Split the differences - Accept part of customer demand. It may limit the satisfaction of the customer but is important to protect the company's interest. It also helps to achieve quick resolution

Add enhancement - This is a bit tricky. Instead of giving what the customer wants, give something which the customer values more, but your cost can be lower than giving what the customer demands. It may incur some extra cost to sales organisation but saves bigger losses. For example, the customer wants 10k discount for a printer but instead of giving this 10K discount salesman negotiated for 12k paper free of cost supply. It can be beneficial for the customer as in any case they need to buy the paper but good for the company as the 12k paper may cost the company 7K only.

Make a Trade-off - Salesperson agreed to give what customer demanded but in return got something valuable for him/her.

This can be the best way if permissible. Here the customer and the salesperson both get the benefits.

For example, the customer wants 10% discount. The salesperson agreed but negotiated for a higher volume.

Power & Pressure:

What defines the success of a negotiation most? It is the quality of a salesperson to understand the power and pressure game which is an inherent part of any negotiation. The power and pressure are not only on the salesperson but on the customer also. Let me to explain with an example.

If it is at the end of the financial year. The salesperson knows that the customer has no other alternative at this point and the budget can lapse. It is pressure on the customer and power to the salesperson. Now if this order is very big and can be a big loss for the organisation and the salesperson/ organisation may fail to hit the budget then it is pressure on the salesperson also. On the contrary, if the deal does not happen it is not a big issue for the customer, as they can use the fund for something else, which can be a power for the customer. Examples can be unlimited and we may find them from our experience. In such cases, the inside information plays a major role.

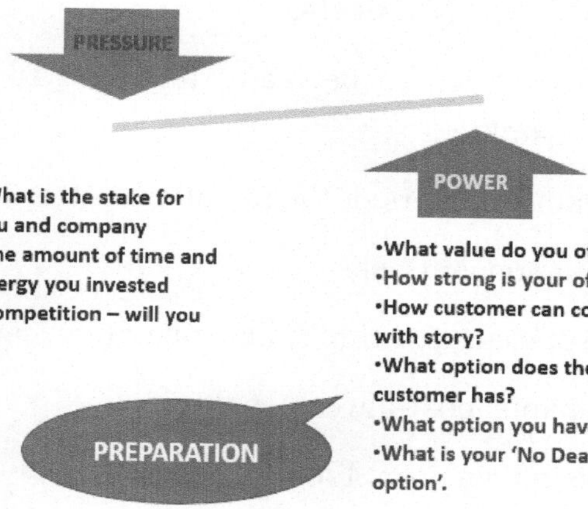

Let me to hail a practical example – it was in one of the IITs and the value of the deal was about 1cr 30 lakh. The customer was pushing for 1cr which I could have easily accepted. But I had the information that they have the budget and they decided to go for it based on my long term relationship and work with the actual user of the machine as a trusted partner. The committee told me, either accept 1cr or the case will be dropped. So, I had to pretend, which is required sometimes, to prevent such adverse situations. I asked for a little time to go out and discuss it with my boss. They agreed. I went out and did nothing and come back after a few minutes and said, 'My boss did not agree as we have already given a rock-bottom offer. However, if they can release the order before I return, I can provide 5L discount and can convince my boss when the order is in hand'. They not only agreed but were happy as they could bring the benefit of 5L for the institute, which I could see on their faces. Not only I closed the case in our favour, but got the order in the shortest time. It is also important not to accept the customer's demand easily even it is within the salesperson's capacity, which surely creates doubt in the customer's mind that they could have got a better price or terms. Some amount of drama is good.

Deal with Different Mindsets:

Also, salesperson need to be ready to deal with a different mindset. For example -

One or few team members of the negotiation team –

Can go for a personal attack.

Unrealistic proposals and threat like 'take it or leave it'.

Raise new demands post-agreement.

Provide abuse information. Lie.

In all these cases salesperson should use intellect and not emotion. The need is to focus on the solutions. To take utmost care so that there will be no slip of the tongue or any wrong word used. Also, instead of getting angry or puzzled, we need to think that bad people are basically fools, less logical, less intelligent (subject knowledge is not intellect) and easy to convince (read defeat) if one can refrain from landing in their core area of arrogance. Talk logical.

Lost Order:

Now comes the hardest part. Order lost! Is it a big failure? Surely, because the salesperson worked on it possibly for months, spent company money and now it is lost. This is a common feeling but is not necessarily a bad thing. If one can do expert negotiation and then lose an order it can be good for the company and may be good for him/her also. This means the order could have been damaged more either initially or in long term.

Walkaway:

A walkaway can be a good option. When? When no alternative works either for customer or salesperson.

Should the salesman show dissatisfaction during the walkaway? Yes, and it should be in a diplomatic way. Never show anger or frustration. Never close the door and sometimes a lost case comes back in a sweeter way. Never damage a relationship. However, expressing regret and showing disappointment is good as we are all human beings. It shows a genuine nature as well as makes the customer sympathetic. Explain the decision nicely as to why the salesperson wants to walk away. Also, one needs to show that he/she is interested to work together in future.

I tried to capture the vital information though this is my two days training program and it is not possible to explain it in short. I shall be happy to conduct the training for the benefit of the youngsters not expecting much own benefit. If you feel you can contact me.

However, I believe budding salespeople can get immense benefit going through this article.

VIVEKANAND – BEYOND A YOGI!

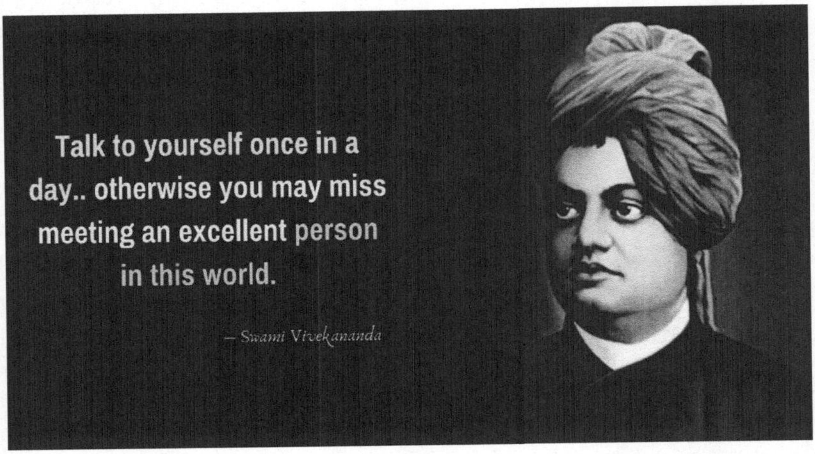

A thousand-page book may not be enough to explain one of the world's all-time great philosophers but let us know something which can motivate one to learn more about him. Learning Vivekananda means learning the inner truth, the purpose of life. But for common men like us, the below facts can give great confidence, and set the right attitude and zeal to do something beyond one's limit. He is as contemporary as today not only in the social atmosphere but in the corporate world also, where many strategies are based on his thought.

These are just a few drops from the ocean of knowledge that Vivekananda gave to the world in his short life of only 39 years.

'Who are you?', Thakur Ramakrishna Paramhansa Dev Asked.

'I came to you to explore that who I am. Who am I?'

'Come my child. I am waiting for you for decades', Thakur replied.

This discussion was between Ramakrishna Paramhansa Dev and Naren in their first meeting. Later the relationship became global, one of the most spoken relations of religious excellence.

Naren? Yes, you know him as Vivekananda.

It is impossible to capture Vivekananda in thousand pages and I am trying to give some glimpse in one page. So I need to be in fast forward mode. Only, a few interesting matters I am presenting below which are related to Swami Vivekananda.

He was born in a poor Kayastha family. The situation became worst when his father died. Do you believe that Vivekananda could lie? Yes, he did! There was a time when they did not have enough food in the family, he used to say his mother that he was going to attend an invitation to a friend's house. So that his mother could have a full meal. And he was spending time on the road and returning empty stomach. He was loving his mother a lot.

Vivekananda was unique in many ways. He advises the young people to go to Football grounds than to mandirs (temples) as building character and good physique is primary at that age. He said, 'Jibe prem kore jei jon, sei jon sebiche ishwar' (Those who serve others serve the Lord, in the true sense). So, praying does not make any sense unless we are kind to people and especially deprived people.

It is unbelievable that how a person can travel across India, such a vast country that too on foot and some sponsored train tickets, in his short life of 39 years. That included his phenomenal journey to the bottom dot of our country, Kanya Kumari (presently known as Vivekananda Rock). As well as the well-known US travel and his phenomenal talk in the World's Parliament of Religions.

Many great people came in touch with Vivekananda at a different times and became a follower and admire of Swami

Vivekananda. Some of the names are Bal Gangadhar Tilak, Subhas Chandra bose, Bhagini Nivedita, Roma Rola and Jamshedji Tata. The list is endless. Jamshedji Tata met him when they were sailing from Yokohama to Vancouver in the same Ship. Jamshedji Tata told Vivekananda that he was going to Europe to bring technology to India. Vivekananda asked him why he needs to go to Europe to bring technology. He told him that if he really wants to serve India he should take initiative to develop science and technology inside the country, as we do not have a dearth of intelligent people. The advice touched Jamshedji so much that in return he established the Indian Institute of Science in Bangalore which was the first big initiative to develop science inside the country and later contributed in a big way in this direction. The seed that Vivekananda planted in his mind bore fruit. Roma Rola said that if people want to know India he/she must know Vivekananda first.

When he went to the USA, it was by courtesy of his followers like the King of Ramnad, Khetri etc. King of Khetri also suggested his name as Vivekananda before he left for the USA. Besides his knowledge, he had a good hold of English, was an excellent orator and had a godly voice.

When he reached the USA, he was highly disappointed to learn that no one without credentials from a bonafide organisation can participate in that conference or deliver a talk. However, he managed to get an opportunity but the organiser allotted only 2 minutes. Two minutes to cover Hinduism which evolved through thousands of years! However, he accepted it. This is one of the best examples of never miss any good opportunity, accept it even if it is small and make it big.

He started with, 'Sisters and Brothers of America'. The entire audience was shocked. 'Who is this gentleman and what he is saying?'. They were habituated to hear salutations like 'Hi',

'Hello', 'My Dear Friends' etc. But this gentleman was referring to them as a Brother and Sister. They started clapping and with a long standing ovation, the allotted two minutes were over. However, the organisers also were surprised and understood that this man must have something unique. So they allowed him to continue. And rest is history. After this incident, Vivekananda also delivered hundreds of lectures across the USA on invitation before he returned to India.

One day he was walking in the street in USA and a few locals started mocking him observing his uncommon saffron dress. Then going a step ahead, one of them asked him why he did not dress like a gentleman. The reply that Vivekananda gave them not only made them spellbound but astonished anyone ever came across it. He said, 'In your country, the tailors make you a gentleman but in our country, our character makes us a gentleman'. What a response, still gives me goose bumps!

I feel it is enough as of now and let us not to dilute the feeling...' character makes us gentleman'.

#SubrataHalder

New Delhi, India.

M- 9999715748